ANIMALS

Elephants

by Kevin J. Holmes

Consultant:
Glenn Goodman
Assistant Curator of Elephants/Carnivores
Zoo Atlanta

Bridgestone Books
an imprint of Capstone Press
Mankato, Minnesota

Bridgestone Books are published by Capstone Press
151 Good Counsel Drive, P.O. Box 669, Mankato, Minnesota 56002
http://www.capstone-press.com

Library of Congress Cataloging-in-Publication Data
Holmes, Kevin J.
   Elephants/by Kevin J. Holmes.
   p. cm.—(Animals)
   Includes bibliographical references and index.
   Summary: An introduction to elephants, covering their physical characteristics, habits,
food, and relationship to humans.
   ISBN 0-7368-0495-1
   1. Elephants—Juvenile literature. [1. Elephants] I. Title. II. Animals (Mankato, Minn.)
QL737.P98 H66 2000
599.67—dc21   99-051630

Editorial Credits
Erika Mikkelson, editor; Timothy Halldin, cover designer; Kimberly Danger, photo
   researcher

Photo Credits
Cheryl A. Ertelt, 8
Craig Brandt, cover
Diane Bos, 6
Frederick D. Atwood, 10
Joe McDonald, 18
Leonard Rue Enterprises, 14, 20
Michael Turco, 4
Visuals Unlimited/John D. Cunningham, 12; Will Troyer, 16

1 2 3 4 5 6 05 04 03 02 01 00

Table of Contents

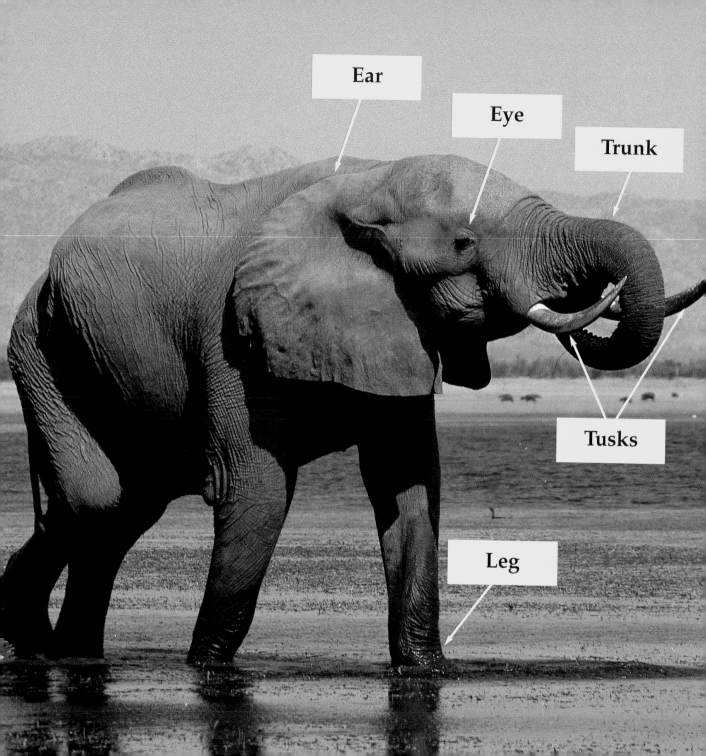

Ear

Eye

Trunk

Tusks

Leg

Fast Facts

Kinds: The two kinds of elephants are the African elephant and the Asian elephant. The Asian elephant also is known as the Indian elephant.

Range: Elephants live in Africa and Asia.

Habitat: Elephants live in forests, on savannas, or in the bush. The bush is the area between the grasslands of the savanna and the forest.

Food: Elephants eat leaves, grass, fruit, and plant roots.

Mating: Male elephants compete with each other for the right to mate with a female. Male elephants are called bulls. Female elephants are called cows. A cow often can choose her mate.

Young: Young elephants are called calves. A calf weighs about 200 pounds (91 kilograms) when it is born. A calf usually drinks its mother's milk for two years.

Elephants

Elephants are the largest land mammals on Earth. Mammals are warm-blooded animals with backbones. Mammals feed milk to their young.

Scientists believe that more than 25 different kinds of elephants once lived on Earth. The woolly mammoth was an ancestor of the elephant. This animal lived thousands of years ago. The woolly mammoth had long hair all over its body.

The two elephant species living today are the African elephant and the Asian elephant. The Asian elephant sometimes is called the Indian elephant.

Elephants have large heads and bodies. They have thick legs. Elephants have large ears and long, flexible noses called trunks. Elephants have thick, gray skin.

The size of adult elephants keeps them safe from predators. Lions, wild dogs, crocodiles, or hyenas may attack young or injured elephants.

African elephants have larger ears than Asian elephants.

Appearance

African elephants and Asian elephants look similar. But their size and their ears make it easy to tell them apart.

Size is the most noticeable difference between African elephants and Asian elephants. African elephants are larger than Asian elephants. Male African elephants weigh as much as 13,000 pounds (5,900 kilograms). Male Asian elephants weigh about 10,000 pounds (4,500 kilograms).

The ears of African elephants and Asian elephants also look different. African elephants have large ears. Asian elephants' ears are much smaller.

The elephants' bodies also are different. Asian elephants have an arched back. African elephants have a slight dip in the middle of their back.

Both species of elephants have long, curved teeth called tusks. Female Asian elephants do not have tusks. Both male and female African elephants have tusks.

Asian elephants have darker skin than African elephants.

Homes

Elephants live in warm climates. Asian elephants live in Southeast Asia, South China, Sri Lanka, and India. They live mainly in forests.

African elephants live in the central part of Africa. African elephants' habitats are forests and savannas south of the Sahara Desert. The flat, grassy savannas provide elephants with plants to eat.

African elephants also live in the bush. This area lies between the savannas and the forests. In the bush, elephants can eat the grass of the savannas. They also can rest in the shade of the forests.

Today, most elephants live in national parks or reserves in Africa and Asia. People set aside these lands to protect elephants from hunters. Few elephants can survive in the wild. Hunters shoot elephants for their tusks. Farmers kill elephants that destroy the crops they plant.

African elephants find much of the food they eat in the bush.

Trunks and Tusks

An elephant's trunk and tusks make it easy to identify. An elephant's trunk is a very long nose and an upper lip. The trunk has thousands of muscles. These muscles allow the elephant to twist and stretch its trunk in almost any direction.

The trunk has many uses. An elephant uses its trunk to breathe, smell, eat, drink, and shower. An elephant will die quickly if it cannot use its trunk. A finger-like projection is at the end of an elephant's trunk. This projection helps an elephant pick up small objects. Asian elephants have one finger-like projection. African elephants have two.

An elephant's tusks are important to its survival. Tusks are actually long teeth made of ivory. They continue to grow as long as the elephant is alive. Elephants use tusks for fighting. They also use their tusks to dig for plant roots. During the dry season, elephants use their tusks to dig for water.

Hunters kill elephants for their ivory tusks.

Food

Elephants are herbivores. Elephants eat leaves, grass, fruit, and plant roots. Each day, an elephant may eat between 330 pounds (150 kilograms) and 500 pounds (227 kilograms) of food. Elephants eat for almost 16 hours each day.

Elephants use their tusks to tear the bark off trees. Elephants sometimes knock down whole trees in order to eat the leaves at the treetops.

Elephants must drink a lot of water. An adult elephant drinks about 50 gallons (190 liters) of water each day.

Elephants also need salt. Elephants usually get salt from the plants they eat. But plants sometimes do not contain enough salt. Elephants then search for salt on rocks. Elephants use their tusks to break off a piece of salt to eat.

Elephants spend much of the day eating and drinking.

Mating and Young

Male and female elephants mate to produce young. Female elephants are called cows. Male elephants are called bulls.

Each year, bulls have friendly fights with one another. These fights are called "musth (MUST) battles." These battles sometimes can injure or kill an elephant. Musth battles determine which male is strongest. This male earns the right to mate with the females of the herd. The bull may chase a cow for hours before mating with her.

A young elephant develops inside the female elephant's body. The female elephant gives birth 22 months later. This pregnancy is the longest of any animal on earth.

A young elephant is called a calf. A calf weighs about 200 pounds (90 kilograms) when it is born. The calf drinks its mother's milk for the first two years of its life. A calf learns how to use its trunk during these years.

Bulls fight to determine who will mate with a cow.

Herds

Elephants live in herds. Each herd is led by one female called the matriarch. The matriarch is one of the oldest elephants in the herd. The other elephants depend on her to help them find food and water.

Elephant herds usually have 20 to 50 members. Elephants work together to take care of sick or old elephants. When a calf is born, each member of the herd helps to raise it. A cow allows any calf to drink her milk.

As female elephants grow, they remain with the other females. Female elephants often spend their entire lives with the same herd.

Males leave their mothers when they are about 13 years old. They live alone or with other males. Bulls travel with the herd long enough to mate with the cows.

The entire herd cares for elephant calves.

Elephants and People

People change the land that elephants live on. Farmers clear trees to grow crops. Destroying trees leaves the elephants without enough food to eat. Elephants also have less space to roam freely. The destruction of their habitat causes the number of elephants to decline every year.

People have hunted and killed elephants for centuries. Hunters sell elephants' valuable ivory tusks. People make jewelry and other items out of ivory. Today, it is illegal to hunt elephants and sell their tusks. But some hunters continue to kill elephants.

Some people in Africa and Asia buy elephants to do work. Elephants carry people and goods. In Asia, people train elephants to clear trees out of forests. People then can farm this land.

People use elephants to travel and carry goods.

Hands On: Elephant Walk

Elephants live in herds. Elephants often form a line when they travel. Elephants use their trunks to hold on to the tail of the elephant in front of them.

What You Need

Five or more players
Two cones or markers
Cassette or compact disc player
Large playing field
"Baby Elephant Walk" music by Henry Mancini

What You Do

1. Choose one player to start and stop the music. Divide the rest of the players into two teams.
2. Place the markers 50 yards (46 meters) in front of each team. Each team should start at the same end of the field.
3. Each team should pick a leader. The rest of the team should line up behind the leader.
4. Join hands with the player behind you by placing your left hand between your knees. Your left hand is like an elephant's tail. Your right hand is like an elephant's trunk.
5. Start the music. Both teams should begin walking toward the markers. Each time the music stops everyone must stop walking. The team that reaches the marker first without letting go wins the game.

Words to Know

ancestor (AN-sess-tur)—a member of a family or species who lived a long time ago; the woolly mammoth is the elephant's ancestor.

bush (BUSH)—an area of land between the savanna and the forest

mammal (MAM-uhl)—a warm-blooded animal that has a backbone and feeds milk to its young

mate (MATE)—to join together to produce young

matriarch (MAY-tri-ark)—a female elephant that leads a herd; the matriarch often is the oldest elephant in the herd.

musth battle (MUST BAT-uhl)—a fight between male elephants to determine which one will mate with a female

predator (PRED-uh-tur)—an animal that hunts and eats other animals

savanna (suh-VAN-uh)—flat, grassy land with few trees

Read More

Harman, Amanda. *Elephants.* Endangered! Tarrytown, New York: Benchmark Books, 1996.

Travers, Will. *Elephant: Habitats, Life Cycles, Food Chains, Threats.* Natural World. Austin, Texas: Raintree Steck-Vaughn, 1999.

Useful Addresses

Elephant Conservation Research
106 East Hickory Grove Rd.
Bloomfield Hills, MI 48304

The Elephant Sanctuary
P.O. Box 393
Hohenwald, TN 38462

Internet Sites

The Elephant Sanctuary
http://www.elephants.com

Wild Lives—Elephants
http://www.awf.org/animals/eleph.html

Index